A Song Just for Me

For Margaret –
Blessings from
Kiki

A Song Just for Me

Mary Kiki Wilcox

2014 · FITHIAN PRESS, MCKINLEYVILLE, CALIFORNIA

Published by Fithian Press
A division of Daniel and Daniel, Publishers, Inc.
Post Office Box 2790
McKinleyville, CA 95519
www.danielpublishing.com

Book design: Eric Larson, Studio E Books, Santa Barbara, California

Distributed by SCB Distributors (800) 729-6423

LIBRARY OF CONGRESS CATALOGING-IN-PUBLICATION DATA
Wilcox, Mary Kiki, (date) author.
A song just for me : stirred by music to conversation and compassion / Mary Kiki Wilcox.
pages cm
ISBN 978-1-56474-556-9 (pbk. : alk. paper)
1. Music therapy for older people. 2. Music—Psychological aspects.
3. Nursing homes—Recreational activities. I. Title.
ML3920.W53 2014
615.8'5154—dc23
2013035821

For my friends and teachers
in the Health Center

Contents

Introduction

I TELL THESE stories as I remember them. They happened in the Health Center of my senior community, where I take recorded music, on a CD player, to the residents in the Assisted Living and Skilled Nursing Facilities. We listen together, as a group, in our weekly "Mostly Music" sessions, or individually, in their rooms. And we talk—about whatever comes, whatever moves them.

I'm not certain what it is that happens when we listen to music and talk together. I do know that what I see in their faces and what they choose to talk about touch me deeply. These people become my friends. They become my teachers.

I try to play their favorite music. Usually they, or members of their families, tell me what they enjoy. If no one is able to do this, I turn to my rolling luggage carrier, which holds the CD player and a collection of favorites, and choose segments from a variety of music. Then I watch for a response—usually a smile or a movement of head or arms or sometimes toes under the covers. I know then that I am getting close to feelings and memories.

How did this come about? When my husband, Wally, died in 1999, I needed to find something to bring joy back into my life, to give me purpose. Maybe I could be helpful at the nearby elementary school. I could teach a child to read, as I had done for twenty years in San Francisco as a teacher and principal. Or perhaps I could volunteer at Stanford Hospital. When I mentioned these options to a soul-friend, she suggested I choose work to help myself, as well as to help others. She added, "Do something that takes you to the mountaintop."

I pondered—would there be something I could do with the residents in the Health Center that would really make a difference to them, and to me? I remembered that when Wally was in the Health Center I would bring a book of poetry to read to him. After a few days, people from neighboring rooms began to come into his room, quietly, with their walkers and wheelchairs, and listen. And sometimes, afterwards, there was conversation.

So I tried again. I read poetry to the residents, and waited and watched. Not the lofty peak yet, I concluded.

Then I had a dream.

Everyone in the world is in mourning. Deep losses. Scenes of devastation. Despair all around. People don't seem to know what to do for themselves or for each other. There is no time to ponder the situation. They need help now. I direct everyone to go to the Greek Theater in Berkeley. Then, using a CD player on center stage, I play music.

I begin with the first movement of the Brahms Requiem—the lower strings and the chorus, hardly audible at first, unfolding gently. "Blessed are they that mourn, for they shall be comforted." I watch the people sitting in silence, allowing the music to comfort them—some in tears. At the end of a row of seats, I notice a young African American girl. She smiles serenely, joyfully, as she listens. The music offers her solace.

The dream clarified what I was to do. It was music that had been part of my life since the age of six. Although music was my widowed father's solution to his concern about the whereabouts of his five children after school hours, I remember music lessons as my grounding and my joy. And now it was music that was going to take us all—the bed-bound, those with walkers and wheelchairs, and me—to the mountaintop.

A Song Just for Me

Always

ELVIN AND HELEN sit together, holding hands. Helen, with multiple health problems, including dementia, lives in the Assisted Living Facility of our senior community. Elvin, still in the apartment where they lived together for years before Helen's illness, visits her every day. And when he does, they hold hands.

For an entire year I've been passing Helen's room. When she is with Elvin she looks comfortable, contented. When alone she seems a bit wary, not quite settled.

"Hello," I say. "I'm Mary. I'm glad to see you this morning." Helen frowns—or perhaps doesn't see me clearly. I suspect she can't speak very much, but my hope is maybe for a nod.

"Would you like to hear some music, Helen? In this little carricr, I have a box that can play lots of different recordings. Maybe I have something you would like to hear." Helen closes her eyes and drops her head to her chest.

I leave but I don't worry about her. After all, she has Elvin. Sweet, faithful man—he stays with her every night until she falls asleep. Then he returns to his own apartment—and is with her again the next day.

A few weeks ago, I asked Elvin to tell me about what Helen

enjoyed doing when she was able, when she could remember. Among the several things mentioned was the word "music."

"Like what?" I asked.

"Oh, I don't know. All kinds. But mostly she likes hymns. Her favorites. You know, she used to play the piano. Helen was a music major in college."

The next day I walk into Helen's room, past her questioning gaze, and plug in my CD player. Very softly I start to play "Abide With Me." And, joining the Mormon Tabernacle Choir comes Helen's faint alto voice, "...fast falls the eventide." Her first words to me. We smile at each other and I play it again. She watches carefully as I push the little buttons on the CD player.

Next time I visit I play a Chopin nocturne. From curiosity to recognition, she smiles. Nodding with the music, she says to me, "My mother used to play this piece." We play another nocturne. No smile this time, but watching, waiting. She's not played this one, I figure. But surely this waltz will be familiar. And it is. Now Helen is talking—not just words to the hymns. "I played this one," she says. "Not very well though. But my teacher helped me with it. Never could get 'The Minute Waltz' in a minute."

I tell her about my sister who, as a young girl, played it in a recital. She couldn't quite remember the ending, so kept repeating the piece over and over. Her very kind teacher told the audience that she played with feeling. But our family still calls it "The Six-Minute Waltz." Helen smiles. She understands.

Elvin is with Helen the next time I stop by. We begin with the hymns that are familiar. She hums along, as does he.

"Reminds you of your childhood, doesn't it, Helen?" he asks.

"Uh-huh. Lovely."

I play another hymn and then some Chopin. Elvin nods off for a moment. When he wakes up, he tells me about Helen's injections for diabetes and some new medication they're trying.

After a few visits I suggest a Schubert impromptu. "Oh yes, I like him," she says. I am no longer surprised to hear her speaking. She leans close to me, as though she's about to reveal something personal, and whispers, "If Elvin comes in and starts to talk during the Schubert, well, you know, it's okay. He doesn't understand about music the way we do. And the hymns are fine too. They're his favorite kind of music, you know."

When the three of us are together a few days later, Elvin and Helen reminisce about their courtship. Elvin asks if I knew that Helen was a Methodist preacher's kid, and that he was one of those Louisiana Baptists. The word got around that there were some real pretty girls in the Methodist youth group. So Elvin and his pals decided to attend. "Helen was the prettiest one of them all," he says.

"Well," Helen laughs, "once I saw *him*, he didn't have a chance. Married sixty-four years." Elvin smiles, especially pleased, I think, because she remembers.

But then on the following day, I find Helen wandering in the hallway alone, looking confused, disturbed. She recognizes me. "Elvin knows we're expecting guests for dinner. I have everything all ready, nice and hot. But where is he?"

"I don't know," I say, "but if Elvin told you he'd be here, he will be. Let me walk back to your room with you, Helen." As I leave her room I see Elvin coming from the nurses' station. "Not one of our good days," he says. "But Mary, do you have a minute? I have a question."

Elvin asks about a different kind of music. He's not sure Helen will remember, but it's their favorite song from way back in the forties. Did I remember "Always"?

"Yes," I say, "I'll try to find it."

I see this as a good time to look through the collection of audiotapes people have been giving me this last year—labeled "Oldies."

The next morning, as I enter Helen's room, Elvin stands to bring my chair closer to theirs. "Please don't get up," I say. "I can only play this one if you promise not to stop holding hands."

So, with a bit more volume than usual, we hear Deanna Durbin, accompanied by a full string section and a touch of alto sax, singing, "I'll be loving you always…"

Helen lifts Elvin's hand, places it on her cheek, and keeps it there as Elvin speaks the words, "Days may not be fair, always. That's when I'll be there always." As the song ends, Helen kisses his hand.

Finally, Carmina

PLAYING RECORDED MUSIC for the residents in the Health Center is my happy task as a volunteer in the "Mostly Music" sessions in our senior community. But I've never been totally successful at explaining this to Abigail—who, in her mid-nineties, with her imposing presence and commanding voice, perceives herself to be, if not leader, then certainly, co-leader. She likes order and has expectations for all of us.

She tells the group of Health Center residents who gather each week to listen and talk about music, "It is permissible to talk when you come here, but only..." she pauses, noting someone's inattention, "...but only during the applause after a piece is played. And then, just to your neighbor on your immediate right or left."

Abigail's expectations for herself are that she be prepared when I ask for suggestions or requests for future sessions. Her expectations for me are that I meet these requests without delay. This I am able to do for the most part, except for the most recent of Abigail's requests, Carl Orff's *Carmina Burana*.

From the way she adjusts her posture in the wheelchair to even greater breadth, I sense that she is about to stir things up.

Orff's secular oratorio for orchestra and chorus is based on poems that lampoon the Church. Some say the poems were written by defrocked monks in the thirteenth century. They are set to a motley selection of drinking songs with themes of spring, love, wine, and sex—in other words, drinking, gluttony, gambling, and lust.

When I first heard it in my college days, I felt smugly adult as I read in disbelief that these earthy chants of wild abandon were considered to be serious classical music. It is no wonder that *Carmina Burana* was never mentioned in my Catholic high school music classes—and only once in my college years. I learned about it from a boyfriend, who suggested one day that we exchange favorite records. He gave me *Carmina Burana,* and I gave him Bach's *Goldberg Variations.*

Abigail is beginning to show impatience with my delay in providing this request for what she is now calling her "very favorite piece—ever." But I am having difficulty trying to figure out how to introduce this music of the erotic and ecstatic. How will the other residents respond? Would it be exciting, or at least interesting for them? Or would the suggestive text and the rhythmic complexities of the percussive, changing meters find the shocked listeners calling for their aides and making a quick exit in their wheelchairs and walkers?

Maybe I could play this intricate music with the volume down so it would be heard at a *mezzo forte,* not *fortissimo.* But what would a movement called *"Inebriated Scherzo"* sound like when played softly?

Finally I choose one movement I think is sure to please, *Il Trutina,* the one exquisite, tranquil aria, in which the soprano soloist prepares to give her life to her waiting lover. Even though it is only two minutes long, my hope is that this movement will please Abigail, as well as the others. And it does. The group, everyone, responds with applause. As the room grows silent again, Abigail announces, "If you think this is good, just wait until you hear the rest of *Carmina Burana.*"

"As lovely as that, dear?" she is asked.

"Hardly," Abigail laughs. "The rest is a hoot. There's a part with everybody in the percussion section—we're talking about how many timpani?"

"Eight," I mumble.

"Yes. Plus drums, cymbals, castanets, and glockenspiels— more than one—all playing at the same time! And lots of brass. Three full choruses. It'll spin you around, leave you remembering your irrepressible youth, your days of wine and...well, you'll see."

There is an uncertain silence.

"Naah, think I'll pass," says one of the two men in the group. "How about the one—we haven't heard it in a long time—about the sultana whose husband doesn't kill her off because he wants to hear the rest of the stories she's telling him? Remember that part about the ship coming from the far horizon and the violin playing that real pretty song?"

"Yes, yes, *Scheherezade*," the others join in.

Abigail says no more. She sits in stunned silence. The grand figure of Abigail is subdued, more like that of a little waif. Even in the sessions that follow there is no protest from Abigail, not once, about the chatter that occurs during the music.

Our group is just not the same. I want my co-leader back again.

Abigail and I devise our own plan. I will not play *Carmina Burana* for the group. One night after dinner I will go with my CD player to her room in the Assisted Living Wing of the Health Center. We will close the door. And then play at high volume—I must remember that Abigail is hard of hearing—the entire fifty-nine minutes of *Carmina Burana*.

At the arranged time for the orgy, I arrive at her door, knock, and wait.

After a few moments I hear her voice: "Do come in."

I enter.

From the wheelchair by the window in the far corner of the

room I am greeted by—yes, it must be, *it is* Abigail, made up as I've never seen before, in anyone in or out of the Health Center:

Her hair is freshly set and back-combed into an exuberant bouffant. Over her left ear blooms a full, multi-layered red rose, no doubt from the Health Center garden. Her face glows with powder, rouge, and purple eye shadow, and is framed by dangling silver earrings. Strands of pearls, several of them, encircle her neck. Cologne—no, perfume—definitely perfume, fills the air. And, she wears a freshly laundered hospital gown.

"Thought I'd dress up for the concert," she says.

A Time to Reap

"WHAT MUSIC WILL it be today?" Marge asks. In spite of heavy pain medication her voice is surprisingly animated this morning. I see energy in her face when I enter her room.

"Would you like Schubert's 'In Spring'?"

My friend Marge, artist and poet, closes her eyes and listens to the song about youth and love in the spring. The youth knows such a spring cannot return, but the memory will remain always beautiful. A poignant melody with a hypnotic piano accompaniment which is even more compelling, if possible, than the melody.

When the music ends, Marge says, her voice barely audible, "Sometimes music is so beautiful, it is almost unbearable."

And then, as though the thought is just occurring to her, she tells me there is a promise she would like to keep. Would I help her?

Some time ago she told her friend Adele, whose room is also in the Health Center, that she would be visiting her. But then, the worsening pain and diminishing energy made any thought of moving from her bed unthinkable.

This morning is different, and Marge has not forgotten. "Today is the day," she tells me.

Adele is not more than thirty yards from Marge's room. With the help of two aides, Marge is lifted from her bed to a wheelchair. As we attempt this transition, Marge's face reflects the awareness that, as good as this day may be, she is unable to assist her helpers. Even the breath within this very thin body is heavy.

We pause and rest a bit before beginning the move toward Adele's room. Once we are on our way, Marge's eyes become alive with anticipation.

"I hope this is a good time for Adele," she says.

"Shall we ask before we enter?"

"No," she chuckles, "let's surprise her."

We arrive at Adele's open door and go right in. Adele is alone. As she turns and sees Marge, her peaked face brightens. "You came!" she says. "You told me you would come, and you did."

Marge smiles and nods. "Yes."

I move Marge's wheelchair close to Adele's bed. They continue to smile at each other in silence, as though recognizing each other over and over. Nothing more is said.

I think maybe they would like some private time together. I offer to refill Adele's water container for her, and I leave the room for several minutes. When I return, I find them sitting quietly, as they were when I left. They are a tableau of two gentle old friends, welcoming each other's light, sharing their wisdom and their peace. They look up and invite me into their sanctuary.

I help Adele with her drink and offer one to Marge.

"Our cocktail hour," Marge quips.

"Oh my, and at this hour of the day!" Adele laughs and they raise their Styrofoam cups.

As I take Adele's water from her she says, "Mary, you are a good nurse."

"Oh no," I say. "I'm too klutzy to be a nurse."

"No you're not. I'm the one who was really uncoordinated," says Adele, who served as a colonel in World War II and then as head nurse at the Palo Alto Medical Clinic. She tells us about the time she bumped into a rolling hospital cart and knocked over an entire tray of medication.

"No one was more klutzy than I," says Marge. "My mother used to tell me my problem was that I kept falling over my own feet. And I really did that. Not an easy thing to do, you know, tripping over your own feet."

For a few more moments they continue sharing klutziness stories. Then they pause and lapse into another prolonged silence. What is happening between these two friends during this quiet interval? Maybe connections too deep for words: knowing how much they've meant to each other, allowing themselves to be grateful, now needing to let go.

In my own silence, I feel grateful for the friendship of these two women, for the humbling and uplifting gift I receive as I sit with them. How few of us are offered the gift of being with those whose days, whose moments, are limited. Surely a time to reap.

I find myself wondering which of these two friends is the more frail, which we will lose first.

Marge reaches for Adele's hand. "We don't want to tire you, Adele. I think it's time for us to go."

They speak about another visit when Marge has a good day again, and we begin our way back to her room.

Although visibly tired, Marge offers an unhurried "hello" to each person we pass in the hallway. She motions for me to pause in front of a watercolor on the wall. We've passed it many times before. As we move away Marge smiles, her gaze lingering on the picture's mysterious light on the hillside.

When finally settled in her bed, she says with contentment in her voice, "Maybe we could listen to just one more piece of music before I sleep?"

"Something special you'd like to hear, Marge?"

"Oh, I don't know, play something—something that tells me how beautiful the world is."

A Song Just for Me

I WONDER HOW it will be with Sara today. Will I know enough to listen and not talk?

So I whisper, "Want to talk, Sara?"

Her eyes remain closed.

"Or some music?"

After a few moments she looks at me. She says nothing and closes her eyes again. I'm thinking maybe I should come another time.

Sara is in the Skilled Nursing Facility. I can see that she has already had her breakfast on a tray and has been bathed. After this morning routine, I suppose one could be ready for another nap.

Sara stirs. "Stay," she says.

We wait together a few moments and then, slowly pondering my face, she says, "Sing me a song."

I pause for a moment. Somewhere between my warmed heart and stifled laughter, I confess, "Sara, in my entire life, no one has ever asked me to sing her a song."

"Sing me a song."

"Any particular song?"

"You choose."

I think about Sara's favorite recordings. There's the traditional spiritual, "Somebody's Calling My Name," sung by Kathleen Battle. Sara loves the soft, persistent pulse of the bass accompanying the moving, subdued call, "Hush, Hush."

Or Edith Piaf's singing of "La Vie En Rose." A few months before Sara's decline, she told our Mostly Music group about living in Paris as a young teacher and attending a performance by Edith Piaf, who was called "The Little Sparrow." Edith, dressed in black, walked alone onto the enormous darkened stage, and began to sing. It was as though, in her song, she was reliving the pain and sadness of her early years.

"By the time she was finished," Sara said, "everyone in the theater was crying. People just couldn't hold back their tears."

These are surely not songs I could sing to Sara this morning.

Her third favorite, "The Boys of Piraeus," from the movie *Never On Sunday*. I remember Sara keeping time with every beat, her toes dancing beneath the sheets. But that was the one we played on light-hearted, cheerful days. This doesn't seem to be one of those either.

Now, from my own lips, I hear myself saying the words, "I see trees of green, red roses too. I see them bloom for me and you, and I think to myself..."

Sara comes in, right on the beat, "What a wonderful world."

I continue, "I see friends shaking hands saying 'how do you do.' They're really saying..."

"I love you," Sara responds. And then, not remembering the words, we both la-la-la our way through the rest of the song.

On a storage shelf in the Activities Room, I find a large-print copy of "What A Wonderful World" and give it to Sara. As I leave her room, she is reading the lyrics to herself. When her friend, Joe, comes to help with her dinner in the evening, they sing together "What A Wonderful World."

Sara died peacefully three weeks later.

In the Mostly Music group, we honor the lives of our friends with some of their favorite music. I am always impressed—amazed, really—with how willing and respectful the Health Center residents are at these moments of celebration and connection, regardless of the level of memory difficulty they may be having.

As we are playing music for Sara, I notice Anim, our very capable and beautiful aide from Cameroon, writing something hurriedly on a scrap of paper and slipping it to me.

> Hi Mrs. Wilcox,
> Could you please play a song in remembrance of Ms. Harriet Collins? I was her caregiver and she passed away about an hour ago. I don't have any particular song suggestions but something fun and loud (brass instruments) with presence would do fine. She was a wonderful lady, full of life and she loved to listen to the sports channel.
> Thanks. Anim

From my collection of favorites in my luggage carrier, I pull a Louis Armstrong CD, and for Harriet we play his version of "Mack the Knife." We hear plenty of brass, especially Louis's trumpet and his song—unabashedly upbeat—about the collection of bodies whenever Mack's in town. Harriet would smile at Mack the swinger, getting away with murder. Even though Harriet was blind and deaf, today's music she would have heard. Perhaps was hearing it at this moment.

"That was a very good song for Harriet," says her friend, Mary. "But for me, when I die, what I want you to play is Eddie Cantor singing." She provides us with a sample:

> *If You Knew Susie Like I Know Susie.*
> *Oh! Oh! Oh! What a girl*
> *There's none so classy*
> *As this fine lassie*
> *Oh! Oh! Holy Moses, what a chassis…*

But Mary's lyrics are interrupted with other requests. Annie wants "I Can't Give You Anything But Love, Baby." Beth remembers the plaintive, haunting "Bailero" from *Songs of the Auvergne*, sung by Victoria De Los Angeles. And Jane wants the three hundred singers of the Mormon Tabernacle Choir singing "Amazing Grace." At least five verses, she tells us. Betty chooses Itzakh Perlman playing the *"Spring" Violin Sonata* by Beethoven, all four movements.

Barbara has difficulty deciding (or maybe remembering) which song to choose. The others assure her that a song title will come to her, maybe even today as she hears the other songs. "Just keep listening," they say.

The last request is made by Flora, for Bobby McFerrin's jazzy, syncopated arrangement of "Hush Little Baby," with himself singing and Yo-Yo Ma on the cello. And she wants to follow that with Brahms's "Lullaby." She hesitates, unsure of this combination.

"They would sort of go together all right, don't you think?" Flora asks.

"Everything goes together," says Anim.

Barbara continues to ponder her choice. "Imagine," she says. "A song just for me."

Music for Emma

SUSAN, THE HEAD NURSE, has just put a list of names in my hands. "People in the Skilled Nursing Facility, Mary. See what you can do."

With my CD player and bag of CDs, I walk toward the room of the two men at the top of the list, Mark and Jack. My first visit with the really sick folks, I'm thinking. May I do this right.

"Hello," I say. "I'm Mary. Susan mentioned that you might like to listen to some music with me. Tell me, which one is Jack?" Jack raises his hand. "So," says the other, "that would make me Mark." We laugh.

"What I love to do more than just about anything," I say, "is to sit with people and play their favorite music."

Mark smiles as he puts down his paper. "You mean stay here and listen with us?"

"Yes, if that's all right. Do you have some favorites?"

"Easy," Jack says. "Anything Mozart."

Mark tries but can't remember the tune or the name of a long-ago favorite he used to sing in his youth. I choose, from my portable collection of CDs, a Mozart *Rondo for Piano and Orchestra in D Major*, a spirited, playful piece that invariably has listeners tapping feet and beating time with their hands.

In the middle of the Mozart, an aide comes into the room. She apologizes for interrupting, says that Miss Anderson, the patient across the hall, wants whoever is playing the music to go to her room—*now*. The aide explains to us that she tried to tell Miss Anderson that I was playing for two others at this moment and that she would tell me about her request when I was finished. "But Miss Anderson said to tell you that she wants to have some of what she is hearing—*now*."

I smile, thinking that this person is being complimentary about the choice of music, or maybe even about my volunteer work. We finish listening to the Mozart, and as I unplug the player I remind Mark to write the name of his song, if he remembers it after I leave. "It's okay," he says, "I think I would like to hear some more of that very nice music by that fellow, Mozart."

I cross the hallway and approach this new person, who has been asking for the music and also, I believe, for me.

"So, what took you so long?"

"Hello," I say. "My name is Mary. You are Miss Anderson?"

"Call me 'Emma.' I sure had to wait long enough for you to get here. What are you doing with this music? Why are you doing this?"

I explain that I think the residents who don't have the opportunity to leave their rooms very often would appreciate listening to recorded music. "What kind of music do you like?" I ask.

An impatient wave from Emma. "So why did you go to them, my neighbors, first? Why did you choose them instead of me?"

Wondering how I happen to find myself in such situations, I tell her that from this little CD player I carry around, we can hear all kinds of music, that there is plenty here for everyone.

"Well, you need to know right now, that I am sicker than all of these other people."

In spite of this less than endearing beginning, I do play for Emma. She tells me exactly what it is she wants to hear: Chopin,

Tchaikovsky, and Mendelssohn. "Composers who write melodies," she tells me. I have with me the Itzhak Perlman recording of the Mendelssohn *Violin Concerto in E Minor.*

"Both men, totally acceptable," she says, with a hint of concealed satisfaction on her face. She lies back on her pillows, closes her eyes, and together we listen to the entire concerto. At the end she smiles. "Oh, I feel so relaxed now. So calm."

And then, the Emma I met thirty minutes ago, returns. "So, will you play again this afternoon, or do I have to wait until tomorrow?"

We have difficulty planning a schedule that works for the two of us. She truly wants to know why other people are taking my time away from her. I tell her that I know her illness is serious and I am sorry this is such a hard time for her. But there are others here who are very sick too.

"Piffle," she replies.

She dismisses the suggestion of listening to recordings on her own or on the classical music radio station, explaining that it's just not the same. She wants to listen with someone who loves the music as she does.

"The people on that list of yours—those people probably have never listened to classical music in their lives."

"That's okay," I say. "All music is acceptable to me."

"Not to me."

"Emma, do you remember..." I move close to her and sing into her ear: "'Mairzy doats and dozy doats...'"

"'...and liddle lamzy divey...a kiddley divey too, wouldn't you?'" she laughingly replies, without even thinking. "Okay, you win."

And that is how finally, grudgingly, she accepts the rights of others and a two-session-per-week plan for herself.

In spite of our schedule, our time together is a puzzling mixture of contentment while the music plays and the discontent that follows. I cannot erase the sound of her voice after a session:

"Sheer ecstasy, I tell you. Nothing can be better than lying here and being played to. No pain. None at all." And this is followed with, "I just can't understand what you see in Phyllis." Phyllis is her roommate at the other end of the room, and probably within hearing range. "Why are you bothering with her?"

"She loves music too. As a matter of fact, she likes the same kind of music you like. And she is my friend."

"Well, I question your judgment."

Also during our sessions, she manages to explain to me, in her booming voice, that the doctors know nothing, that the other two women in her room are impossible to get to know—"not that anyone would want to," she adds—and that the help is absolutely useless. After that, she has no difficulty closing her eyes and blissfully allowing herself to be carried to the heavens with the Tchaikovsky *Symphony No. 6*, *"Pathetique."*

Emma is as certain about the music everyone else should like as she is about the music she likes. One day I suggest a Mozart sonata for violin and piano or an aria from a Bach cantata.

"No, no, no. Let's not waste time with little sonatas. Why settle for two instruments when you can have a full orchestra? And certainly no screeching sopranos." She pauses, wanting to say more. "There is something I would so much like to hear again. I wonder if you can help me find it. A tenor aria from an opera by Bizet, I think. I just can't remember the title." Emma does remember that it was beautiful, and that it was her father's very favorite song.

While trying to recall the piece, she talks about her childhood, growing up in a Jewish home, in a mixed community. She tells me about her father's complex personality and his severe manner, especially with Emma's mother. "We kids were never quite sure what his mood would be and why it could change so rapidly. But then, he had such a love for the arts, especially music. I suppose that's how I came to love music too."

A few days later, I am able to find the aria she requested, "I Hear as in a Dream," a love song from Bizet's opera *The Pearl Fishers*. I take the recording to her as soon as I can and read some of the lyrics to her: "I still believe I hear...her voice, tender and deep like the song of a dove..."

Emma asks to have it played again and again. And she weeps.

In the sessions that follow, she speaks about the injustices of exclusion that plague the world, generation after generation. She is aware that most of the composers we are playing have Jewish backgrounds, and she wonders how difficult their lives must have been, because of the bias of our anti-Semitic world. She remembers the prejudice she experienced in her youth, as a second-grade teacher in the Palo Alto public schools, during a brief, childless marriage, and, yes, maybe even here in our senior community. "Something I could feel," she says. "It's real."

For a brief interval our schedule is legitimately interrupted, when I find that I will need to have cataract surgery on my left eye. Emma takes this routine procedure seriously. She tells me, in as kindly a manner as she can, that I must follow the doctor's orders carefully.

She calls me a few hours after my procedure. She tells me she is pleased with the favorable report from my doctor and reminds me, ever so gently, that I am to carry nothing and do nothing for an entire week. I am touched by her interest in my health, and resolve to look only with love upon this lonely, kind woman. The next morning, the day after the procedure, she calls again.

"I hope you're not lugging around that CD player. And are you following the doctor's orders?"

"I am, Emma. Thank you."

A few minutes later, the phone rings again. "Mary, I'm sorry to be such a pain in the ass. Could you come and play some music for me?"

Occasionally I take a week or two off my volunteer work to attend retreats in the silence of nature; sometimes Christian, sometimes Buddhist. Emma tells me she follows no religious rituals, and that she has found no solace in the teachings of organized religions. She doesn't know what to make of my so-called retreats.

"Why would anyone choose to remove herself from the rest of humanity? All of these retreats and meditations—got any answers yet? Just think of all the music we could be hearing during that time."

When I return from my retreat, I find that Emma has had a short bout with flu symptoms. Though she recovered, she now has a more serious recurrence. As we listen to music during her illness, Emma surprises me with the suggestion that maybe we ought to give some of those other neglected composers a chance. And we do. She is quick to comment on how much she had been missing by not having had the young Schubert and Mozart in her life. After hearing the Bach "Sicilienne" from *Sonata in E-flat Major for Flute and Harpsichord*, she asks, "Tell me, how can anyone write something so beautiful? I think I'm ready to grow."

Emma responds to the music, but not to the medication for her body's debilitating symptoms. Her condition worsens.

"I am not getting any better, you know. The doctors have told me. And I know it is so. I'm scared. Talk to me."

I hesitate for a moment, wanting to offer Emma what it is I think she wants and needs, and at the same time to be authentic in our conversation.

"What is your fear, Emma?

"Just not knowing what will happen," she says.

We question whether anyone could really know for certain what does happen.

"So you're not certain either?"

"No, I'm not certain. But let me tell you what I think about today, about right now, Emma. I believe that we are not alone, especially in these difficult moments."

Emma waits.

"I think we're not alone," I continue, "because we listen at a deeper level at these times." I pause. "Emma, I will be here with you as much as possible."

I note a slight smile on Emma's face and realize there is one on mine too.

I am moved by Emma's quietude, by a serenity in her that I have sensed before, but which always seemed to leave her when the music ended. It does not leave her now.

"Mary, would you read me some of those words, or whatever it is, that you would want someone to use with you, if you were dying?"

"Yes, of course, Emma." I reach for my small book of Scripture quotations alongside the CDs in my luggage carrier. "It says here in Isaiah, 'Emma, because you are...'"

"Waaaait one minute," she says with her I-gotcha look. "It doesn't say 'Emma,'"

"But it means 'Emma.' It's you this was written for. Isaiah wants us to think of this as the Lord talking to you."

She rolls her mirthful eyes. "Okay, go on."

I have called you by name, Emma, you are mine.
When you pass through the waters, I will be with you.
And through the rivers, they shall not overwhelm you...
Because you are precious in my eyes, and I love you, Emma.
...Fear not for I am with you.

Emma lies very still. We wait. And then she asks, quietly, "Why would God love me? I don't deserve it."

I hold her hand. "God loves you, Emma. And I do too."

Emma asks that wonderful music be played during her final days, including the little Bach "Sicilienne," she has learned to love so recently. For her last hours, the nurses, aides, and I keep the CD player repeat button going throughout the night. Emma's death is peaceful, accompanied by the "Larghetto" movement of Chopin's *Piano Concerto No. 1 in E Minor*.

A Gift for the Season

BILL AND MIKE share a room in the Assisted Living Facility. Their door is slightly ajar. Not knowing if it is a preference for privacy, I knock and prepare to wait. "Come in," is the quick response. I do, and find Bill standing, completely naked.

"I'm sorry, Bill," I say. "I'll come back in a few minutes." I turn to leave.

"Oh, what the hell," he says, reaching for his robe, "come on in. Let's have some Beethoven, before my roommate returns and I have to listen to his stuff too."

Bill and Mike have a love-hate relationship, mostly concerning politics and music. Mike knows a lot about polkas—any kind. Bill loves the classics, especially Beethoven and Chopin. In the interest of equal time we alternate between the two, not without teasing remarks to each other. Yet neither chooses to leave the room when the other's music is being played.

Bill tells me that as long as Mike is not here now, this would be a good time to ask a favor. Do I sometimes go to a record/ CD store? Would I take this money and buy *The Greatest Polka Hits*, played by Frankie Yankovic?

"I know that collection is Mike's favorite," Bill says. "Maybe on Christmas, we could surprise him with it?"

On Christmas Eve I take the CD to Bill. Mike is sound asleep.

"Oh good! Let's put it on," Bill says, and he begins to remove the holiday wrapping.

"But Bill, don't you want to give it to him yourself?"

"Naah. Put it on now, while he's sleeping. He'll think he died and went to heaven."

Mike's feet awaken first; nimble under the sheets. He yells louder than usual, "Where can this fantastic music be coming from? Now you gotta admit, Bill, this is a lot better than that funeral music you can't possibly like." Bill responds with several rounds of hop-one-two-three. Then, bowing ceremoniously, he presents the CD case to Mike.

Neither is about to offer the other a greeting as sentimental as "Merry Christmas."

What's Going On Here?

ED WHEELS HIS chair into the Activities Room and calls out to no one in particular. "So—what's going on here?"

Hilda makes a place for his wheelchair, next to hers, and says, "Morning, Ed. Well, it says on the board that the first activity is 'Mostly Music.'"

"I don't know how to do that. Do you?"

"Yes, I'll show you. It's not hard. Mary plays the music on her little boom box on wheels, and we listen—she says 'with our ears and hearts.' And sometimes we talk about the music. It's easy, Ed. You'll like it."

"I don't know where I am. Do you know where you are?"

"Yes, this is Emerson House. We're at Emerson House."

"Emerson House? What's that?"

"A place in Palo Alto. They look after us here. It's a good place, Ed. It's our home. You and I live here. Mary lives here too."

"We do? Well, what do you know!" He chuckles. Hilda chuckles too. And so do I, as I set up the CD player for this morning's music.

"But," Hilda adds, "I will only be here for an hour or so. My parents are coming for me soon. We're going home today."

"Tell me again. Where are we now?"

Hilda answers. Even in her own confusion, she looks directly at Ed and has a smile in her eyes as she speaks. How could Ed not feel at ease when he is with her? I ask myself to remember that same compassion for Hilda later in the day or tomorrow, when she may again speak about her parents and ask if they have come for her yet.

After a few more residents have gathered, I tell the group that today we are celebrating the birthday of a wonderful French composer whose music..."

"Oh, I hope it's the one who wrote 'Clair de lune,'" says Hilda. "I think it means moonlight?"

"Yes, yes, and you're way ahead of me, Hilda," I say. "We will play 'Clair de lune' by Claude Debussy, who was born in August, 1862."

"Let's see," says Hilda, "it says on that big calendar that today is August, 2012. So he would be one hundred fifty years old if he were here today." We applaud Hilda who has impressed us with such gems before. Ed gives her an approving poke on the arm with his elbow.

"But just before we listen to 'Clair de lune,'" I say, "I would like to play another piece that Debussy wrote. It was for his little girl, his only child, when she was three years old. Her name was Claude-Emma but her parents liked to call her 'Chou-Chou.' The piece is called 'Golliwog's Cake-walk,' from the suite called *Children's Corner*. Golliwog was a rag-doll character in children's books that were popular in those days."

I tell my little circle of listeners that Chou-Chou could have had a golliwog in her toy collection. She could have made her golliwog dance to happy, ragtime music or maybe she would be dancing to it herself.

"Listen to this jolly, playful tune," I tell them, "written by her father, Claude Debussy, just for his little Chou-Chou."

The syncopated rhythm of the banjo, drum, and piano at the beginning of "Golliwog's Cake-walk" has almost everybody dancing somewhere inside their bodies—keeping time with their arms and legs. And all the while smiling.

A round of applause afterwards.

"Wish I could play the piano like that," Ed says.

"Did you take piano lessons when you were a boy, Ed?" I ask.

"Yes, but I quit. Never wanted to practice."

"Me neither," is heard throughout the room.

I ask if some in the group now wish that they had listened to their mothers who were nudging them to continue with their lessons. Almost all in the room raise their arms.

"It wouldn't have mattered in my case," a lone voice volunteers. "My mother would never have allowed me to stop taking lessons. I told her I had no talent. But she said, 'Maybe so, but you may not stop taking lessons. This is the Depression. And your piano teacher needs the money.'"

"I really wish I had practiced enough to play that golliwog piece," says Hilda. "That was fun. Makes you feel like laughing. And it sure is different from 'Clair de lune.'" Now her voice changes—distant, but tender. "I remember 'Clair de lune' as pretty, beautiful really, just like the moonlight. And kind of mysterious. A little sad—but a good sad."

And with Hilda's introduction, we listen to the recording of "Clair de lune."

There is a warm glow in the group silence, even from those whose usual preferences are the popular tunes from the forties. For a few, the peaceful softness seems to bring on a need to close their eyes and to lean forward in their chairs or over the trays of their wheelchairs, possibly to sleep.

When I witnessed such a response during my early years of Mostly Music, I would ask myself: If all they're going to do is sleep, why am I doing this? Why not just select a few good recordings and press the repeat button? But then, in a very short time, I noticed that with those who were apparently asleep, there was often a movement of fingers, hands, feet, or a slight swaying of the body, and—what touched my heart—an almost imperceptible smile.

And I was aware of something more—my own contentment.

Ever since that first awakening, I ask myself as we listen: Who is to say what is happening here, what is being heard, or what is being remembered at the sound of any music? How could anyone know what might be stirring in the heart of another's moonlight?

Afternoon at the Opera

IS IT DRAMA, romance, passion you want? Something up-lifting? Come to our Mostly Music group in the Health Center Activities Room on Wednesday afternoon. We sit in a circle and listen to music that will do all of these things for us. Especially if it's opera, and especially if it's a love story.

We begin with *Madama Butterfly*.

"So here we are in Nagasaki, at the turn of the twentieth century," I tell my little group.

> Lieutenant Benjamin Franklin Pinkerton is a handsome American naval officer. He freely admits, early in the op-era, that he will take Cio-Cio San, his little "Butterfly," as his wife while he is here in Japan. But when he returns to the United States, he plans to have a "real" marriage with an American wife. Butterfly's love, on the other hand, is different. Her love is forever. No matter that she is re-nounced, even by her own family.

I stop telling the story and wait. The mood in the room is somber and unsettled. But the darkness leaves us quickly, as we fall under the spell of the couple's fervent song of love in the first act.

> *"So many watchful stars...Sweet night of enchantment...Ablaze with love."*
>
> Pinkerton says, "Come, you are mine now."
> Butterfly replies, "Yes, for life."

There is a round of applause. Nods of approval. "Lovely," Janet and Patty say. But not Francesca. In spite of the rapture of the love duet, she doesn't allow the music to dispel her concern for Cio-Cio San's childlike happiness, or her suspicion of the roving Pinkerton. *"Hmpf"* she grunts, "that music is too good for a guy like that."

In the second act, two years later, we find Butterfly and her child waiting for Pinkerton to return from America, as promised. There is a grim I-told-you-so shaking of heads from this group of listeners.

"Well," I say, "most of us in the audience already know what little Butterfly doesn't—that Pinkerton will return. But with his American wife. And only to take his child. Butterfly, on the other hand—she still believes. Listen to her fantasy:"

> *One fine day we will see his ship entering the harbor. I shall go to the top of the hill and wait. And wait. He will call, "My tiny little wife, sweet scented flower," the names he used to call me. All this will happen.*

Some folks are almost believing. Janet and Patty, uplifted by the poignancy of Butterfly's naive joy, seem to be willing it so. But not Francesca, who I'm supposing to be asleep. "No sireee!" She pounds on the arms of her wheelchair. "That rat! Any guy who's gonna treat me like that is out of here. Who does he think he is anyway—God Almighty?"

—

TOSCA is Clara's favorite opera. She is a diminutive ninety-eight-year-old. Two of her could fit into one wheelchair. Once a librarian, she's neat and precise, always on time for the group. Some may think she's prissy, but only if they do not look into her eyes, wide with expectation, eager for the story's music to unfold.

She is an expert at moving her wheelchair in reverse, so as not to face Melvin Green whenever he starts rolling up his trousers to his knees—and then back down again. Clara likes details, like the three ominous chords that tell us that the villain, Scarpia, is up to no good. She listens raptly as Scarpia plots his own gain of Tosca and the murder of her lover, Mario. (And he's thinking all this while in church!)

"What a scene," I say. "Imagine the choir singing the sacred 'Te Deum' while Scarpia, on his knees in prayer, is at the same time planning homicide."

"So good!" Clara's face tells me.

Now, in the next act, Scarpia bargains with Tosca (a mock execution of Mario in exchange for the promise of her favors) and all the while makes sure she—and all of us—can hear Mario's screams, as he is being tortured. Scarpia signs and hands the pardon for Mario to his aide, and immediately takes Tosca in his arms. And what does she do? She plunges a knife into him, with the words, "Thus it is that Tosca kisses." We hear once more the three fateful chords, but this time so very softly, as he dies.

Clara's face is pure satisfaction. She doesn't even notice that Mr. Green's trousers are rolled up again.

The third act takes place on the ramparts of the castle. Mario understands Tosca's arrangement for the mock execution: he is to pretend to die at the sound of the firing squad, and then the two of them will be free forever. But no, nothing goes according to plan. The firing squad shoots and marches off. But Mario doesn't move. Tosca screams, "Mario! Mario!"

The soldiers, having discovered Scarpia's dead body, scurry back to the courtyard to seize her. "Ah Tosca, you'll pay dearly for his life," they shout. "With my own," she cries, and flings herself over the parapet, hurling herself into space. And while all this is happening, the full impassioned orchestra is thundering out this tragic end—the death of both the hero and heroine.

How can I not look at Clara at this moment? Her eyes twinkle with merriment. Full smile. Her grandmotherly hands are clasped in front of her heart.

"Delicious," she says.

—

FOR the opera *Carmen*, I don't even speak the title. With the volume turned up, Bizet's rousing orchestration of the prelude tells it all. Lively festivity on a sunny afternoon in Seville, the gaiety and the drama of the amphitheater interspersed with rousing, tantalizing rhythms. And we too, find ourselves part of the crowd, cheering as we recognize the "Toreador Song," the theme of the dashing bullfighter, and we sing along.

The music is intoxicating, and throughout our Activities Room I hear clapping and tapping of feet. Francesca, smiling and swaying, gets up from her wheelchair without any help, unbuttons her blouse, sways some more, buttons it up again, and sits down. The drama is about to unfold.

"I guess our Gypsy heroine, Carmen, is feeling a little like this too," I say.

Carefree and flirtatious. Carmen now is breaking away from the other employees who are returning to work in the Seville cigarette factory. She moves slowly, seductively, watching and being watched by the soldiers coming from their sentry post into the town square.

Noticing the young corporal, Don Jose, who to this moment is the only one not encouraging her advances, she tosses him a flower. He reaches for the flower and what do you suppose happens?

"He's a goner," says Francesca. "Doesn't have a chance."

"Yes," I say, "he is under her spell. For all time. But not for Carmen. Oh no. She tells us that Gypsy love knows no law, only destiny; that Gypsy love is just for the moment, like a capricious bird that alights only near those who ignore it."

"Right on!" says Francesca. "Nobody gonna mess with her!"

"But watch out for her," I caution. "Listen, here's the toreador's theme again. See, she is already flirting with the handsome bull-fighter, the toreador."

Again the group recognizes his theme, and joins in. They participate a little more loudly each time they hear it.

Don Jose swears his constant love and pleads with Carmen, even at the cost of his military career. And how does she answer? She laughs at him.

Francesca warns, "Trouble ahead."

The day of the great spectacle in the bullring arrives. The chorus describes the finely dressed crowd, the dignitaries, vendors, and bullfighters. And, finally, to much acclaim, the great toreador appears, with Carmen on his arm. But she does not walk with him into the amphitheater. She stops at the entrance. She knows that a desperate Don Jose has been looking for her. Defying her friends' warnings, Carmen tells them she is not afraid. She remains outside where she can easily be seen. A lone Gypsy figure.

"So sad," some say. "Waiting for her destiny, I suppose." Several nodding heads, agreeing. "Nothing can change it."

A tattered, distraught Don Jose appears. He sings of his love for Carmen. He begs her to come back to him, but his pleading is in vain. The more he pleads, the more contempt Carmen shows, throwing the ring he has given her at his feet. She scoffs at him.

"But listen to the music from offstage at the same time," I say. More of our little group join with the large chorus, singing the "Toreador Song" as the crowd cheers the victorious toreador. "The bull loses," says Francesca.

"So," I ask, "after the rousing toreador song, and following the soft expression of love from Don Jose, what would you think if you heard a loud, dissonant blast of horns?"

Francesca again, "Somebody's up to no good. You can bet it's got to be Don Jose."

Yet another loud roar of the crowd from the arena off stage, celebrating again the victorious toreador.

Onstage, the broken, desperate Don Jose can take no more. He draws closer to Carmen and, weeping, plunges his knife into his beloved. "Carmen, I adore you."

"Poor fellow," say Janet and Patty. "She wasn't worth it."

"Sure she was," says Francesca.

I AM beginning to think maybe we need a little less violence in our Mostly Music sessions. Perhaps a heroine who makes the ultimate sacrifice for her lover will be perceived as admirable. I choose a mini-version of Verdi's *Aida*.

"A beautiful Ethiopian slave girl, really a princess," I say. "And Radames, the Egyptian commander-in-chief, is in love with her. He sings to her: "Celeste Aida, heavenly Aida, fair as the sunrise.""

Janet and Patty remember, from their childhood, the old Caruso records of the aria, played often on their parents' wind-up Victrolas.

"And do you know what happens to heavenly Aida?" I ask them.

"Yes, I think she dies," says Janet.

"No, I think Radames, he dies," says Patty.

"Both right," I say. "He is condemned to death for a number of reasons, including loving Aida and not the king's daughter. He is placed in a huge vault, sealed by an enormous stone. And, listen to this, who do you suppose actually chooses to enter the tomb and die with him?"

"Aida!" is the triumphant response.

"Yes," I say. "They die together. What loyalty. What sacrifice. That Aida! Isn't she something!"

"I suppose," says Francesca, "but Carmen! She's my favorite. She's my kind of gal."

Sometimes I wonder—might I be leading my little group astray?

Ich Habe Genug
(I Have Enough)

I REMEMBER HEARING his music for the first time. I have just stepped out of the elevator on the seventh floor of my senior community. The hallway has come alive with beckoning sounds. I follow them to a closed apartment door, from which comes the glorious recording of Johann Sebastian Bach's Cantata, *Vergnügte Ruh (Joyful, Contented Peace)*. I linger, but only for a few moments, knowing I must play this same work from the beginning as soon as I reach my own apartment.

The next time I take this path I hear music again—Bach's *Keyboard Concerto No. 4 in A Major*. The name on the door is Joe Fetzer. My neighbor tells me that this lover of classical music is a retired professor of economics.

When I see him eating alone one day at lunch, I invite myself to his table. "I've been listening to your music," I say. And so begins our friendship and our exchange of classical recordings.

It isn't a simple thing to find a Bach selection that Joe doesn't already have. But I sometimes have the same music performed by different artists. Unless I nudge Joe into expressing his opinion, he rarely speaks about differences in the recordings. He prefers finding something to commend about both versions, and always with enthusiasm.

Well, maybe not always. One evening I decide to listen one more time to Bach's *Brandenburg Concerto No. 2*, the recording I plan to leave at Joe's door the following morning. But he doesn't respond for several days, and then when he does, it is with hesitation. He thanks me for the CD and says he is certain that it is a lovely recording. "But, Mary..." He pauses. "Uh...I hope not to hurt your feelings, but...there is no disc in the album." I laugh, remembering that the disc is still in my CD player.

We find ourselves wondering about this music that touches our core. What does it mean "to touch one's core"? Joe asks, and then says, "One might as well ask why the sunset is beautiful and the sight of an infant so heart-warming."

I learn more about Joe from Sara, his life-long friend who also lives in our senior community. In their younger years, they both were teachers in Alaska. They piloted their own airplanes and traveled to distant places together. Now neither is in robust health. Sara, in the last few months, too frail to live on her own, has moved to our Skilled Nursing Facility.

When I ask her if she would like to listen to music together in her room, she responds readily. She enjoys remembering the music she loved through the years, and offers a variety of requests. Then one day she asks me to select the music. I choose *The Notebook of Anna Magdalena Bach*, which includes pieces by Bach's wife and their children. As soon as Sara recognizes the Bach sound, she reaches for her telephone and calls Joe. She holds the receiver close to the CD player and chuckles as she waits for him to answer. "Joe," she whispers, "it's Johann Sebastian Bach." They listen together. She is smiling throughout the piece, and I imagine that he is too.

Sara grows frail, more quickly than we expect. Occasionally she keeps a recording for a few days, to enjoy with Joe when he visits. Painful as it must be to see Sara's deterioration, he sits with her every evening, as he slowly and carefully helps her with dinner. He shows signs of weariness, but even so, he is there every night and often during the day.

After Sara's death, Joe begins to reveal more of his own diminishing health. He stays alone in his room much of the time, takes most of his meals on trays, and listens to his recordings. Then, gradually, as he grows weaker, there is less music coming from his apartment. Maybe he is in pain, or maybe he is too weary to manage even the remote control.

I am pleased when he agrees to my playing favorite music for him in his apartment. We most enjoy discussing which of our favorites to replay.

The one cantata we both choose without hesitation is the poignant *Ich Habe Genug (I Have Enough)*. As I expect, Joe already knows the story of this cantata, how it was written for the Feast of the Purification, and based on the story of Simeon from the Book of Luke. The elderly priest, Simeon, after blessing the child Jesus in the temple, gives himself permission to openly yearn for his own death:

> *I have enough...I would now with gladness make hence my departure.*

The deep bass voice and the soulful oboe and strings speak to each other in their common yearning. The bass affirms this need to depart:

> *I have enough...Ah! My departure, were it here, with joy I'd say to thee, O world: I have enough.*

In the second aria we are gently rocked into repose, longing for sleep—for death.

Slumber now, ye eyes so weary, fall in soft and calm repose! World, I dwell no longer here...

These two arias we play most often. Although Joe weakens, and his speech becomes more halting, there is still the warmth and gentle appreciation with which he listens to the Bach arias. They become our theme through the following days.

He welcomes the music, but then, gradually, I can see that even listening for short periods of time takes a toll on his energy. I wonder, during these precious dwindling days, if, in the stillness of his sickroom, he might be resonating with something deeper within, something other than music, something more.

The next time I enter his apartment I can see in his eyes that he is expecting me. I begin with the first aria of *Ich Habe Genug*. Joe responds to the plaintive sound of the oboe's opening theme with a faint smile of recognition, which remains with him as he lies back and closes his eyes. When the first aria is over, remembering the possibility in this moment of "the something more," I do not move on to the second aria. I wait in silence. I wait for Joe to lead me.

He does. He leads us both. After this silence, he opens his eyes and speaks, softly and clearly, his last words to me. "Mary, I love this music you have been playing for me. And I can't thank you enough for all you have brought. But now...now... *Ich habe genug.*"

Carolyn's Christmas

"JUST LOOK AT Carolyn's face," Gwen whispers to me. "She's so excited!" It is the morning of Christmas Eve and Gwen, Carolyn's aide, has brought her in her wheelchair to my apartment door.

Carolyn is beaming. Where are the wrinkles, the weariness from assuming the same position for years on end, as a stroke victim often does? Instead I see eyes that are alive, color on her cheeks, a red blouse—indeed a celebration.

This is our planned time together, to watch a videotape of *Great Performances* series in which Renée Fleming, Carolyn's most favorite musician, is featured in a program called, "Sacred Songs and Carols."

Carolyn hoped to watch it in her room in the Health Center last Thursday when it first aired on PBS. Gwen was alerted to turn it on at eight o'clock. But in spite of Carolyn's deep desire to watch, she was unable to stay awake. Not to worry, Carolyn knew it would be recorded.

I remember that Carolyn once mentioned, in as pleasant a manner as one could, that she would be so glad when Christmas was over. "Oh those television shows! I've had enough of Santa coming to town, and that even more irritating one about the reindeer with the nose."

Understandable to feel that way. Carolyn loves classical music. The program we are about to view will include familiar selections by Bach and Mozart, and other classical composers. Although there may be some Christmas carols (Carolyn is Jewish), I'm relying on Renée's selections, and the tenderness in her voice, to carry a message of peace and renewal.

We settle down with tea, holiday cookies, and chocolates. Then we turn on the video. She watches and listens intently as Renée speaks briefly about her childhood, singing in the church youth choir and then later in her mother's adult choir. She comments on Renée's festive beige and black gown, the warmth of her beautiful face, and the clarity of her speaking voice. Carolyn is an artist. She appreciates everything that goes into a performance.

As Renée begins to sing, Carolyn is silent for a long time. Then, noting Renée's effortless transition from very low to a soaring higher register, she smiles and nods. "How," she wonders, "can anyone sing something so technically demanding, and look at ease, as though she's having a wonderful time?"

We stop the tape for a moment before the singing of Berlioz's "Shepherd's Farewell," a new piece for Carolyn. We talk about the shepherds telling the infant Jesus that, yes, he must now leave his little stable. But they want him to remember that if the world out there gets to be too much, too unkind, he could always return to the humble hearth of his shepherd friends. "Thy home be with us," the shepherds say.

We listen again to the tape, to their simple song.

The delicacies on Carolyn's tray are forgotten. We are immersed in the music, by this dazzling soprano voice. Carolyn makes sure I observe Renée's stage presence, her appreciation for the choirs and for the instrumentalists as they support her obbligato. "Every inch a performer, an actress as well as a fine musician, don't you agree, Mary?"

"Yes, I do." In these moments, I am aware that I am the gifted one, gifted with Carolyn's joy.

The last part of the program brings familiar Christmas carols, to which Carolyn listens as attentively as to the earlier classical pieces. Renée then announces that her final selection will be "Silent Night," to be sung in German. This is Carolyn's first language, and I am somewhat uneasy. How will she respond to the words, "Christ the Saviour is born"?

Renée begins *"Stille Nacht, Heilige Nacht…"* The strings in the orchestral accompaniment are soft and pure. And then I hear another voice singing along with Renée. It's Carolyn! She and Renée Fleming are singing together. I turn to look at Carolyn and see that she has tears in her eyes. Still singing, and with tears. "My mother and I used to sing this when I was a child," she tells me.

"In your home?"

"Oh yes. Each year at the Christmas season my mother and I sang *"Stille Nacht"* together. It didn't matter that we were Jewish. Mother had learned, as a young girl, about the celebration of Christmas from a Christian friend."

Gwen returns and pushes Carolyn's wheelchair toward the elevator. Carolyn's eyes are alive, as when she first came. But now they are also glistening, filled with remembrance.

Remembering Carolyn

I ASK CAROLYN how it is, not to be able to use the left side of her body at all. Her response is brief: "Happiest are those who know what it is they cannot change," an old German verse she learned in her childhood.

Carolyn, an immigrant from Germany, has been for the last several years living in our Health Center, the victim of a stroke. She needs to be lifted from bed to wheelchair. She turns the pages of a book only with measured effort.

Carolyn and I listen to recorded music together. And we talk. She wonders, openly and directly, why at ninety-three she is still alive, and then she moves on to something else—a dream that is on her mind. Would I like to hear this dream?

I have thirty-five dollars, all the money I have left in the world. My total balance. I go to the Greyhound bus station and ask for a ticket to wherever this thirty-five dollars will take me.

From her expectant smile, I understand that this is the end of the dream.

"Where will you go?" I ask. "North? South? East?"

"Doesn't matter."

"What will you do when you get there?"

"Don't know."

"Will you be happy there?"

She smiles.

Carolyn's favorite composer is Puccini, especially when sung by Renée Fleming. And there is always Mozart. Bach is less familiar to her and she asks to hear more of his work. She listens, fully absorbed, to the *Air from the Suite for Orchestra, No. 3*. Moving her good right arm over her immobile left arm, she says, "It's beautiful. Like being stroked."

She likes to know the stories behind the music, and the biographies of the artists. I often find her with a smile on her face, listening to opera recordings on her head set, while following the large-print librettos prepared for her by the office staff.

The playing of Jacqueline du Pré always moves Carolyn, but she does not request her recordings very often, having difficulty separating the beautiful music from the premature death of the young artist. "Stricken so early. It's just too sad."

When I ask Carolyn what she thinks about during the long silent hours in her room, she speaks about her childhood, her beloved husband, people who helped her grow along the way (some intentionally, some not) and, she whispers, "I tell myself stories. I see things." She points out a tiny speck in the skin of her forearm. She is convinced that there is life in it. "Just imagine," she tells me, "in this one tiny creature, there is an entire nervous system, all the things that keep it alive. Think of it. In this little speck, the ability to procreate!"

"Yes," I say, "tiny organism—so complex."

My disbelief does not escape her. "I'm talking about this tiny creature," she says, pointing to her arm. "It is alive, you know. And I must be careful not to crush it when I bring my forearm toward me."

Together we speculate about life, birth, and death. One day, looking tenderly upon it, she says, "You know, some people think I'm crazy." She laughs. "I *am* crazy." I touch her forearm gently, we both laugh, and we continue to fondly gaze upon the speck.

Carolyn, the artist, finds beauty wherever she is, in places where I've never looked, such as the curtains around her bed. "Notice the many shades of gray, the darkening where the folds fit closely. How different on this side where there is space between the folds. See how the light changes each fold. It's almost like sunshine." My first lesson in seeing, really seeing.

In her solitary moments Carolyn creates her ideal social state. Her system allows each of us to do what we do best, as well as what we love to do. "It's called following one's path," she tells me. There is no need to exchange currency, only services. "You tailor my over-coat and I will paint your portrait."

And yet, she muses, there is something to be said about the struggle. She reminds me of the effort of the young Renée Fleming, as described in her memoir—slowly and painfully realizing that she is an artist, and must audition with utmost confidence, as though she has already won first place.

Carolyn is so taken with the beauty and artistry of Renée Fleming that she decides to dictate a letter expressing her appreciation. I see Carolyn now as a young girl, writing to her favorite movie star, asking about her schedule for future performances.

To her delight, some months later she receives a response from Renée's secretary, thanking her for her letter and telling about their schedule for the following season. Enclosed are two autographed pictures of Renée. "Look," Carolyn reads aloud, "'To Carolyn with best wishes, Renée Fleming.' For me!" She immediately has them hung on the railing of her hospital bed.

The honeymoon is short-lived, however. On the inside cover of her new CD album there is a photograph of Renée in a revealing décolleté black lace gown. Carolyn, now the artistic critic, is compelled to dictate another letter, informing her no-longer-idol that the photo of the full figure is distasteful and unacceptable. "Ms Fleming," she dictates, "you are a beautiful artist. You do not need to present yourself looking like a whore."

"But Carolyn," I plead, "she's wearing a costume. See, there's Violetta's aria from *La Traviata* in this album. It's the part she's playing."

"Do not defend her," Carolyn commands. "Just send it the way I'm telling you."

A few days later she asks if I have sent the letter yet. She concedes that maybe "no true lady" can be substituted in the whore sentence. The letter is not mentioned again.

A week before Carolyn's ninety-fourth birthday, she develops an asthma condition. She breathes with difficulty and develops a fever. In just a few days she becomes weak and listless—her eyes almost unseeing. Her illness is serious.

Carolyn refuses to be taken to the hospital. She is given oxygen in her room in increasingly greater amounts. When she eats, it is with difficulty. She takes a few spoonfuls, small sips of water, and then not even that.

There is a serenity about her as the doctor, the nurses and aides speak to her. I wonder if she knows what will happen, if she continues to refuse nourishment.

Because of Carolyn's diminishing energy and problematic hearing, our house doctor asks what I believe to be an enormously courageous and honest question. She writes with bold letters on a large piece of paper and holds it close to Carolyn and herself, so they can read together:

MRS. LIPTON, ARE YOU READY TO DIE?

Carolyn nods immediately. A definite, clear statement.

She is no longer urged to eat or drink. Food and liquid are continually brought to her and she is told they are at her bedside. They are left untouched. "Maybe she knows what she is doing," one of the nurses quietly observes, as cold and untouched food is replaced with the next meal.

During the following days, her two cousins from San Francisco and Seattle visit with her. Carolyn is responsive, although unable to speak at length.

Nurses and aides come and go, greeting her warmly as they tell her what they are about to do, sometimes taking vital signs, sometimes, with expert timing and gentle touch, changing her position. They lean close to Carolyn and she can hear the warmth of their voices, as she now begins to go in and out of a coma. I can see the kindness in their eyes, something Carolyn can only sense. As I leave her room at the end of the day, I know there is genuine goodness in this Health Care staff. Something of the sacred, I think.

Although I am not sure if Carolyn can hear music above the oxygen machine's constant throbbing, I continue to play some of her favorite recordings: Puccini arias, the Mozart *Concerto for Flute and Harp*, Schubert impromptus. And maybe because I need to hear it, I play "A Gaelic Blessing."

Carolyn does not belong to any organized faith group, nor does she wish to have a visit with a clergy person. And yet, because through the years I have sensed her spirituality, her compassion for all living things, I decide to read to her from the Old Testament. She remains silent.

I read from Psalm 90.

Lord, through all generations
You have been our strength and our home.
Before the mountains were born

Or the oceans brought to life,
From all eternity, you are...

Maybe she cannot hear this either. Or maybe she can.

I remember that in one of our early conversations she referred to scripture as myths. "Myths that teach, the timeless stories?" I asked. No answer.

Now as she lies still, eyes closed, in a semi-coma perhaps, I say to her, "Carolyn, I want to speak something to you." I move closer to her.

My peace I leave you, my peace I give you,
Trouble not your heart.
My peace I leave you, my peace I give you,
Be not afraid.

For the first time in days, I see Carolyn open her eyes. She looks at me with a radiant calm and nods. I know she hears what she once called myths as timeless stories that are our teachers.

Our music now includes chants, *Kol Nidrei*, and traditional Celtic songs with harp accompaniment. As I hold her hand, she releases hers and places it over mine—holding *my* hand. She then lifts my hand and strokes her cheek with it. I say "I feel as though you're blessing me."

"Yes, many are blessing you."

I do not want her to die alone. I sit by her side for a long time. She now opens her eyes once more, looks at me and speaks, quite clearly, her final words to me. "Look at you! You really should get more sleep!"

She knows why I'm laughing.

It is ten o'clock at night. Carolyn died an hour ago. All is quiet and still in the Health Center. Nurse Jeni and I wait with Carolyn until the mortician comes.

When I hear a slight steady rumble, I look down the hall and see an empty gurney, guided by a large gentle man. He could be the son of Paul Robeson—his sensitive eyes, his respectful demeanor. He moves the gurney slowly to the nurses' station and stands, tall and silent, preparing the paperwork. The few times he needs to speak to Nurse Jeni, his voice is subdued.

He enters Carolyn's room. Calmly and slowly he prepares her body. He lifts her effortlessly and silently to the gurney. I wonder if Carolyn's roommate, encircled by the curtain around her bed, has any idea that this is happening.

Then, almost with a reverence, he moves the gurney out of the room, stops where I am standing, and reaches for my hand. "I am sorry for your loss." He turns and with the same dignity, begins to move the slightly audible gurney down the deserted hallway.

An aide steps out from a patient's room. "Goodbye, Mrs. Lipton," she calls. The procession of Carolyn and her kindly guardian continues, and another aide steps out and joins in this loving farewell.

The gurney turns at the end of the hallway. I hear another voice in the distance, fading away now, "Good-bye, Mrs. Lipton."

Come Dance with Me

...God who only knows four words
And keeps repeating them, saying:
"Come dance with Me."
Come
Dance.

—Hafiz

IT'S THE FIRST Wednesday of the month and Noëlle, in her long flowing gown, sweeps into the Activities Room for her hour of improvisational dance. With outstretched arms, she greets the residents already seated in the large circle. Even those with solemn expressions touch her hands, sense her warmth, and find themselves returning her smile. For this Mostly Music group, the dance has already begun, although I've not yet turned on the CD player.

Noëlle dances in bare feet and always with a scarf or shawl, which becomes a playful partner—sometimes to enfold an infant as she gently sways to Brahms's "Lullaby," or to adorn the shoulders of a coquettish maid.

Noëlle likes to look deeply into the eyes of each person, one at a time. It's as though they are celebrating each other with their hands, shoulders, nodding heads—and, always, laughter. And then she may break away to the larger circle to dance alone for the entire group, which by now has grown to include those standing in the hallway, visitors, and delivery people passing by.

On this September day, we honor the earth and its harvest. Noëlle is wearing seasonal colors, variations of earth tones, subtle browns and soft mauve. Often someone in the group will ask about her dancing costumes, some of which she creates herself. Today she tells us she is wearing the dress of her grandmother, someone she admires. We grandmothers in the group enjoy the image she presents as she moves into the first selection.

The music is "Autumn" from Vivaldi's *The Seasons*, and Noëlle becomes the farmer dancing joyfully in our midst, embracing us, her plentiful harvest.

Then the music shifts to Ella Fitzgerald singing "Early Autumn." Once Olivia in her wheelchair hears the trumpet take over the melody from Ella, she stands, extends and waves her arms to the sky, reaching higher and higher. "Sweet feet," she says, "I could kick the chandelier."

When Noëlle begins to sway back and forth with Eleanor, I notice Olivia motioning to me from across the room. Eleanor has been receiving extra nursing care these last weeks and I think Olivia may be concerned about her stamina. When I reach Olivia, she whispers, "I just didn't want you to miss this. Look at Eleanor's face. She's smiling!" We've not seen Eleanor smile in a long time. I don't know who raises my spirits more—Eleanor reveling in her *pas de deux* or Olivia appreciating Eleanor.

Noëlle tells me, "I dance differently here, more so than at any other place. You know, I'm not drawn to 'stir' people, even if they are mostly sedentary. Rather, together, with very little movement, we simply feel the stillness in our midst."

Today, as Noëlle ends her time of dance with us, she mentions Michelle, who has been missing our sessions the last few months. I explain to her that Michelle is now very frail, and that it has become increasingly difficult for her to be moved out of her room.

"Do you suppose," she asks, "it would be all right if we went together to her room, and I danced for her there?"

Michelle lies pale and motionless on her bed. But now, as Noëlle enters, I see in her face happy surprise and gratitude. I believe she senses Noëlle's total readiness to be with her.

"Oh, I like your space," says Noëlle. "Your light. The pictures. May I look at them?"

Michelle watches as Noëlle moves slowly from picture to picture. Seeing Noëlle's lithe, disciplined body, how could Michelle not remember her own vigorous youth, the young girl who loved riding horses?

"These paintings—they're yours! they're beautiful!"

"I'm glad you like my room." Michelle's voice is halting, but clear.

"I do, especially your paintings."

Noëlle continues to comment on Michelle's art.

As I set up the CD player, I ask Michelle what music she would like to have.

"Mozart," she responds.

I know this means Mozart's *Laudate Dominum*. It is her favorite, the text from the psalms, and she remembers that I always have it in my carrier.

After a slow, lyrical introduction on the strings, we hear Cecilia Bartoli's deep, sustained tones:

O praise the Lord, all ye nations. Praise Him, all ye people.

Noëlle stands at the foot of the bed. She is still, but her eyes are warmly embracing. As the theme repeats and the full harmony of the choir joins in, Noëlle slowly moves toward Michelle and then to the wider space around her, energy gradually building with the music—rising, soaring even higher to the walls and the ceiling.

It seems Noëlle is wanting to touch all the parts of Michelle's world and beyond—losses and sadnesses, joys and blessings that have been lived and felt in this room.

Cecilia Bartoli and the psalmist continue:

His merciful kindness endures forever.

Noëlle circles the small space of five or six feet around Michelle's bed, offering a fluid, seamless prayer. She moves, as though on an endless platform, toward and away from her, giving and receiving. I wonder, how could Michelle—how could anyone, watching Noëlle's grace-filled silhouette—not fully sense the heartbeat in these moments?

As Cecilia Bartoli repeats Mozart's exquisite, final *Amen*, Noëlle slowly falls to her knees at Michelle's side, where she remains until the music ends. We are once again in the silence. Each of us, I believe, with our own internal music.

Michelle reaches for Noëlle's hand. "I think you can do anything you want to do in your life."

Noëlle whispers her thanks and asks, "May I touch your head?" She holds Michelle's head with both hands and they are again in silence.

Michelle smiles. "I feel better now—I used to dance too. I remember how much it meant to me. How I loved it. Thank you."

Noëlle bows in return.

Something Beyond

"LISTEN WITH ME to this piece of music," I tell my little group sitting around our CD player. "It's called 'Larghetto,' the slow movement from Mozart's *Piano Concerto No. 24.*" The solo piano without orchestral accompaniment very softly introduces the opening theme, almost childlike in its simplicity. But now, a slight distraction from the hallway, and the group turns its gaze toward the door. Ruth in her chair is being wheeled into the Activities Room by her aide. It is her first time with this group.

Usually after the initial smiles and nods, the group's attention returns to the music. But this time no one turns away from Ruth. Although obviously very weak, she sits in an upright position and slowly, gradually, extends her arms, reaching out toward the music, toward the CD player. She is looking for something in the distance. Or is it somewhere nearby? Her eyes, deeply intense, are perhaps even more beautiful because of her slight, wasted frame.

The simple, poetic "Larghetto" has never before seemed so poignant. I selected it, intending not just to have the group listen to another beautiful work by the young Mozart, but rather to sense the tranquility of this ethereal prayer. Ruth seems to know this, and she holds her arms outstretched throughout the entire movement. The others in the group quietly watch. So do I.

As the "Larghetto" ends, Ruth withdraws her arms, but as soon as the next movement begins, she reaches out again into the sound. Usually, after a movement or even a short piece, the group applauds, eager to show appreciation, or for the sense of camaraderie it gives them. But not on this day. The residents sit in wonder and watch Ruth in silence.

I truly believe that I am not the only one who is aware that something of the mystical is present in our little circle. I ask myself, how is it possible that these residents, believed by some to have "no quality of life, nothing left," can be so aware and sensitive to Ruth's responsiveness? They are transfixed. They are under her spell.

During the next month, Ruth's aide brings her to the group only two times. She listens with the same intensity. Sometimes she holds her hands clasped in front of her, but her haunting, seeking expression remains the same.

Then, Ruth is no longer brought to the group. Her nurse says that being lifted from bed to wheelchair now causes her too much pain. She sleeps most of the time. I take music to her bedside. "It's no use," I'm told, "she can't hear anything."

But she does. Even with eyes closed, her face tells me she is aware of something beyond. As I leave her bedside, I whisper to her that I will be back in a few days. From her lips, I read a silent *thank you.*

I continue to visit Ruth, but after a while I find myself playing more often for those who open their eyes, who smile, who talk to me.

When I learn that Ruth has died, I feel as though I have abandoned her in her distant space. And now I no longer have the opportunity to offer her solace. Why did I not play for Ruth more often? Did the responsiveness of those who could talk to me make

the difference? Were their words of appreciation part of my deci-
sion to play more for them than for Ruth?

Or, I hesitate to ask myself, do I too believe the words of those
who would see no quality of life in her, who believe that nothing
is left? I like to think not, but it is a question I continue to ponder.

Thomas, Elizabeth, and Bach

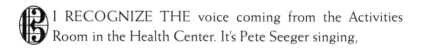 I RECOGNIZE THE voice coming from the Activities Room in the Health Center. It's Pete Seeger singing,

I've been working on the railroad
all the live long day.
I've been working on the railroad
just to pass the time away.

The group, holding songbooks with large print, follows along with Pete.

But not Thomas and Elizabeth. They hold the songbook but they do not sing. Their eyes are without focus, someplace else, beyond this room. Where? How I wish I knew.

Thomas, formerly a Stanford Professor of History, has had multiple health problems. Elizabeth, who needs help getting from place to place, describes herself simply as "mother of four." But her eyes tell me of more, something I know little about.

As I pause at the door of the Activities Room, the recreation assistant notices that I have my CD player in tow. "I guess this isn't their most favorite kind of music," she says. "Would you like to play something else for them?"

An aide and I push Thomas and Elizabeth's wheelchairs down the hallway, looking for a quiet space. We choose Elizabeth's room. There is only one other person in it, and she is asleep.

We settle ourselves around the CD player, our little community of three—and I invite one more: Johann Sebastian Bach. Thomas smiles, recognizing the lively opening bars of the *Concerto for Oboe and Violin in C Minor*. He sits tall and alert in his chair. Elizabeth leans back, smiling in anticipation.

I start to adjust the volume, thinking it may be too loud for the sleeping roommate.

"No, no," Elizabeth says. "Leave it as it is. It will not wake her up." She leans toward me and whispers, "You know, some of this wonderful sound will ooze through her pores, right into her body."

Thomas immediately responds to the echoes of Bach's compelling rhythms. He holds up his arms and begins to conduct. He knows how to use larger arm movements to increase the orchestra's volume, and small, delicate hand motions for a softer passage. His head, working together with his left hand, leans toward the orchestra for clean, precise entries. After a particularly clean attack, the phantom musicians are rewarded with an acknowledging smile. For fuller sonority, he vibrates his left hand over his heart. Thomas and the orchestra—an excellent ensemble.

The only time Thomas seems to forget the beat is during the breathtaking slow movement, when the violin and oboe take turns with the soulful theme. They intertwine. They speak tenderly, as though saying to each other, "Oh, see, how beautiful you are." Sometimes they answer each other. Sometimes they finish what the other is saying.

This is when Thomas's appreciation for each turn of phrase moves him to tears. He weeps openly, unashamedly. Elizabeth respectfully averts her eyes, honoring the moment.

As this movement comes to a close, Thomas knows what to expect. Now he's back on the podium. He takes a deep breath.

Once again he is the director, in command of the animated first measures of the final movement.

But just then, his nurse Tracy enters. "Mr. Thomas, I've been looking all over for you. Time for your blood test." I realize that I should have notified the staff. One wouldn't expect them to look for a man in the women's ward. "I'm sorry," I say, "I should have told you where we were."

Tracy says she's glad we're having a good time.

"We really are," says Elizabeth. "This is our healing time. One forgets one's troubles."

Thomas, all this while, is encouraging the lively dialogue between soloists and orchestra. Continuing to conduct, he offers Tracy his left hand for the blood test. As she leaves, he mouths, "Thank you."

Peaceful listening resumes. But Tracy returns almost immediately. The blood test reveals that an injection is needed, now.

Thomas, the only one not dismayed by her words, smiles at this news.

Without a pause in his conducting, he extends his left arm. She says, "I need your right arm this time, Mr. Thomas."

Not missing a beat, Thomas passes the baton to his left hand and extends his right for the injection. He continues to conduct with his nodding head and left hand to the completion of the injection, and to the final dramatic closing of the Bach *Concerto for Oboe and Violin in C Minor.*

Tracy joins us in our applause. Elizabeth calls out, "A fine performance, Mr. Conductor."

From his wheelchair Thomas bows from the waist to his appreciative audience, and to composer Johann Sebastian Bach.

Schubert and Ice Cream

"AH, SCHUBERT AND ice cream. Ice cream and Schubert."
I have just turned on my CD player to the Schubert *Impromptu*
Number 3 in G-flat. Anna takes her first teaspoon-taste of this afternoon's serving of vanilla ice cream. With a youngster's delight
she savors each taste, each sound, exclaiming, "My two favorite
things."

Anna receives her care in the Skilled Nursing Facility, but she
impresses me with her energy, her lively conversation about music
and her family.

Widowed twice. Each husband was the father of a son. There
is some difference in age between the sons, of course, which Anna
considers to be part of the reason they did not form as strong a
bond as she had experienced with her siblings through the years.

Jon, the older son was away at college when his younger
brother, Ted, was growing up. And now, both sons, with families,
have positions in distant parts of the country. She regrets that they
do not often see each other.

Anna shows special interest in Franz Schubert's story, this pro-
lific composer who died at thirty-one, leaving to the world music for piano, chamber groups, liturgical chorus, symphonies, and
songs—six hundred of them.

She shakes her head when I talk about Schubert's father interfering with his passion for composing music by insisting he become a schoolmaster.

"But the young composer was not to be denied," I say to Anna. "During the school day (or so the story goes), the eighteen-year-old Franz just couldn't allow himself to lose the themes racing through his head and heart. So what do you suppose he did? He wrote them, as they came to him during the day, on his starched cuffs."

"So good," she laughs. "He figured out a way."

She enjoys the questionable tales about Schubert's escapades after leaving the classroom and his home—how he enjoyed playing music in the company of his friends. Because of his capacity for drinking, they called him "The Sponge."

Although Anna seems alert and cheerful during our sessions, the nursing staff observes a gradual decline in her condition, and Anna's family is alerted. Within twenty-four hours Jon and Ted arrive.

During our first conversation, I sense a genuine caring between the brothers and love for their mother. I am touched by their sensitivity as they gently tell me that her illness is terminal.

Anna calmly accepts her prognosis. She refuses to consider my concern about intruding on this precious family time together. She counters with, "It's true that I love these two guys more than anything, but Schubert and ice cream are close seconds, so please keep up with your part of my favorite things." And I do.

Jon and Ted help select the Schubert pieces for the family music time. Their unanimous vote is for the exuberant *Trout Quintet* for strings and piano. This spirited and humorous piece is based on the playful Schubert song about the capricious trout and the angler. It ends with a brief mini-drama, as the heartless fisherman unfairly stirs the brook and muddies the water. The agitated trout is no longer able to avoid the rod. We notice that Anna smiles more often and eats her ice cream a little more quickly during the lively fast movements.

Of course the brothers love the music too. They are their mother's sons. They join her with portions of vanilla ice cream as well.

Anna's condition worsens slowly. When it looks as though her final days may happen later than expected, both sons immediately agree to stay on as long as necessary.

Anna sleeps longer than earlier in her illness. When she is asleep, or in need of more rest, Jon and Ted, always together, fill their days and nights with animated conversations, and with explorations of their old childhood haunts.

Anna weakens. Talking at any length with her sons makes increasing demands on her energy. More of her vanilla ice cream is now left melting in the little dish by her side. Still, we continue with the sounds of Schubert, listening mostly to her favorite lieder, "Night and Dreams" and "To the Moon." We are all puzzled by her amazing resistance to letting go. What, we wonder, is that something that is keeping her alive beyond the doctor's expectations?

Then, one morning, in the presence of her sons, Anna leaves this life.

Jon and Ted plan a warm celebration—pictures of the young Anna, her husbands and growing sons. They share stories and memories, as well as music, including the Schubert lied "Wayfarer's Night Song II," composed to Goethe's words:

>...*Soon you, too,*
> *will be at rest.*

As the last guests leave, Jon and Ted bring champagne and large servings of vanilla ice cream for themselves and me. They sit next to me at the uncleared table and tell me they have a theory about why Anna took longer than expected to die.

"Mom knew what she was doing," Ted says.

"She won!" says Jon.

"Won! Won what?"

They chuckle at my confusion.

"Mom had a way of making things happen the way she thought they should happen," Jon says. "She never could give up on things that didn't go the way she had planned."

I wait.

"Mom always wanted us to be really good friends," Ted explains. "And we did too. But when we were kids, we just weren't around at the same time."

"So," says Jon, "it's taken us a while to figure out what she was up to. We think she delayed her final hours intentionally, making sure we had the chance to get close, to bond—as she must have always wanted for us. She gave us the time to do that."

"Resourceful to the end," says Ted.

Together we drink to Anna. We drink to Anna's long farewell.

"And," says Jon, "a toast to Schubert and ice cream."

Her Mother's Daughter

"HELLO, EVERYBODY! Wonderful to see you again." She throws kisses. Embracing the many old friends in our music circle, she makes her way toward her mother's wheelchair.

Barbara comes from Nebraska several times a year to visit her mother, Molly—and the rest of us too, we've come to believe. Molly, typically demure and gentle, finds herself chuckling, totally responding to her daughter's Carol Channing effervescence. She seats herself next to her mother. Now, with her arm around Molly's shoulders, in the midst of our laughter, she nods in my direction and invites me, "Oh yes, please do continue with the music."

She enjoys all kinds of music, including the classics, which her mother must have played for her in her childhood. Today Molly is fingering the Chopin "Nocturne in D-flat" on her lap, in the same tempo, complete with trills and runs as in the Artur Rubinstein recording we are hearing. I sense Barbara's delight, as she notes how Molly and Rubinstein simultaneously pause, just for a heartbeat, before a particularly beautiful passage. Mother and daughter surely sense the beauty of this moment. We, the other residents and I, know that something precious is happening between them.

Barbara also introduces us to one of her generation's popular tunes, Foreigner's "I Want To Know What Love Is." When her husband is visiting along with her, they dance together in the middle of our circle, many of us clapping and chair-dancing as we watch.

On this day she asks if I have some flapper music, maybe a Charleston? Oh yes, a number of our group remember; they would like that too. When I bring in the CD the next day, Barbara springs to her feet. With high-kicking, fast-walking steps and the hot-jazz timing of the early twenties, she gives us a seductive, provocative Charleston.

"Wow!" I pretend shock. "Dancing like that! In front of your mother!"

"And who do you think taught me?" she replies. Molly's laughter, an admission of guilt, has us feeling like young things again.

Barbara's visits every few months never fail to spread cheer to everyone she encounters in the Health Center. But then, more often than in the past, there are illnesses, some more serious than others. And with each recovery, Molly takes longer to regain some of the strength of her old self. Her diminishing health is apparent to Barbara during her visits. Not surprisingly, they use their time for conversation, favorite things to eat, stories to remember, and, of course, music. Molly gradually realizes that her memory is also beginning to fail and she becomes less responsive.

One brisk autumn day, at a time when Molly's awareness is especially poor, we are pleased to see Barbara at the door of the Activities Room. Perhaps her being in town may bring a smile to Molly today. From the expressions of the others, that seems to be their hope too. Barbara smiles briefly at our group and goes directly to the chair next to her mother.

"Mama!" Barbara embraces her. "I'm here, Mama. It's Barbara. I'm here!"

Molly looks in the direction of her daughter. Her eyes are open but she appears unseeing. A fixed, questioning gaze. She does not move. No change of expression. Does she not see her daughter?

"Mama! Mama, I just got here. I've come from Nebraska to see you." Barbara holds Molly's hand, kisses her cheek, touches her face, her hair. Molly continues to look at this very nice woman sitting at her side, who is embracing her, stroking her. She studies the face—what is it that this stranger can be wanting?

We sit in silence, our little group, feeling as sad as Barbara, wanting so much for Molly to recognize her daughter in some slight way. Barbara in our midst must know that all of us watching are filled with love for mother and daughter. We have forgotten our own aches and disabilities. It is they who are fully in our hearts, in need of our comfort.

I turn up the music a little. A slow movement, a soothing Schubert piano sonata. I think that maybe I should play something familiar to Molly and Barbara. Maybe I should...but Barbara is ahead of me. In her effort to reach her mother, she is stroking her arms, rubbing her hands, whispering, loving her. And then Barbara finds herself placing her hand in front of her mother's face, by her mouth.

And just at that moment, Molly's eyes begin to come alive! What is Molly experiencing as her daughter holds her hand to her mouth? Might she be recognizing the familiar scent of her child in her arms?

The entire room is rapt in wonder. Is Molly really recognizing her daughter? Molly looks into Barbara's eyes. Wondrous recognition. She shakes her head, in disbelief that Barbara is sitting there in front of her.

"It's you!" she says.

"Yes, Mama. It's me!" Barbara cries. "I just arrived from—Oh, Mama—It's so good to be here with you."

Molly is now kissing Barbara. Everyone in the room—crying and smiling at the same time.

I Didn't Want Them to Miss the Mozart

FRED LIVES AT one end of our Health Center. Lydia lives at the other. She can walk; he cannot. She remembers yesterday; he remembers days of long ago. When I pass their open doors in the morning, I sense aloneness, isolation.

A few hours later, I see the small and slight Lydia, now almost regal in bearing, proudly pushing a contented Fred in his wheelchair. She has a smile on her face as she leads from behind. I don't know how they manage to find each other, but just watching them together makes the rest of us feel kinder, happier.

Lydia greets her neighbors, Jean and Roger, also on their way to the Activities Room, where our Mostly Music gatherings take place. "Favorites today," she calls out. "I think Mary is going to play some of your favorite thirties and forties music, and some of our favorites too."

There's not much disagreement about what we will hear on Favorites day—any music requested in the last month or two that moves our group to applause and smiles, or to tears. We note these moments and know we'll get to hear them again soon.

The first time Fred requested Beethoven was in earlier, healthier days. He speaks very little now, but we know, as he responds to the music, that his choice is still Beethoven. This morning we begin with the opening movement of the *Moonlight Sonata.*

Fred and a few others close their eyes as they listen. His soft expression tells me he is being carried to a gentle, peaceful place. As the piece ends, he opens his eyes, nods to me, and smiles. I respond with a nod and a smile. This opening slow movement is indeed a beautiful piece.

Fred nods and smiles again and waits, expecting...yes, I understand now. He would like me to continue with the next movement of the *Moonlight Sonata.* "I'm sorry, Fred," I explain, "but this album has only slow movements. But, Fred, I will bring you the entire *Moonlight Sonata* tomorrow. We will listen to all three movements together."

Fred does not understand. I repeat slowly. He still cannot understand and attempts to help *me* understand in the only way he can—he sings the theme of the second movement. It is unmistakable, "Ta ta, ta TA...ta ta, ta TA..."

The next day, listening to the entire sonata, we have no trouble communicating. As it ends, a beaming Fred raises both arms, his gesture of victory.

Jean's request is "Bill," from the musical *Showboat.* This has been her choice a number of times before. She exudes joy when she hears this song. It is inevitable that someone—today it's Lydia—is surely going to ask her about this person, Bill. "Who is Bill?"

"No, not my husband," Jean tells us. "Bill was my first love." There is a silence in the room. Of course, we're all thinking about her husband, Roger, sitting right there next to her. She helps us through our awkward silence. "Oh it's okay," she says. "Roger liked him too. In fact we named our first son after him. He's Bill too."

Jean also loves the song from the musical *Mame,* by Jerry Herman, because of its "mesmerizing banjo beat and the catchy lyrics," she says.

You coax the blues right out of the horn, Mame.
You charm the husk right off of the corn, Mame.
You make the black-eyed peas and our grits, Mame
Seem like the bill of fare at the Ritz, Mame...
We think you're just sensational, Mame.

As the banjo continues strumming, Jean moves her walker to the middle of the room, gets up, and begins an improvisational solo dance. Before I can even try to prevent her from falling, Megan, our ever-alert activities director, becomes her graceful dance partner, the two of them bending and swaying until the end of the tune.

Roger requests "Vilja" from Franz Lehar's operetta, *The Merry Widow*.

The beautiful and wealthy widow is being courted by the many suitors in the little kingdom of Pontevedro. At her fashionable party, she sings a love song. But wait! She, recently widowed, and a proper lady—how can she do this? But it's all right. She does not sing about her own love affair. Rather, she sings about a forest nymph, who falls in love with a mortal, the young helpless shepherd. Most of our group join in the singing of the chorus to the lovely maid of the woods.

Roger rolls his wheelchair away from the group toward the CD player and me. He whispers, rather apologetically. "Mary, I don't mean to be disrespectful. I hope you understand what I mean when I say that the merry widow in this story reminds me of you. Well, you know, I don't mean that all the men around here are courting you."

"That is true. They're not," I laugh.

"But, Mary, you come in here every week with your smile and wonderful music, and you make us happy. You are our merry widow."

Roger rolls his chair back to the circle and we proceed with Favorites.

— . —

The last Favorites are Lydia's. Two violin-piano sonatas by Wolfgang Amadeus Mozart—one, written at age six and the other
twenty years later. We begin with the early two-minute sonata fea-
turing a melody on the violin and a simple piano accompaniment.
The instruments then alternate parts, piano now with the violin
melody, and the violin playing what was just heard on the piano.

"Imagine," Lydia says, "this little Wolfgang composing in his
head, and thinking—these miracles, I have to learn to put them
on paper."

Now we play a deeply expressive movement from *Sonata in
C*, one of many written in Mozart's twenties. Lydia looks around,
pleased that the others are also enjoying the delicate dialogue so
exquisitely performed on the two instruments. And then, at the
most poignant moment in the sonata, Lydia gets up and leaves the
room. She returns a few moments later.

When the sonata ends, Lydia is very still, holding a kindly
motherly gaze on the CD player.

She turns to the group.

"Do you want to know where I went?"

"Yes," we say.

"Well, I went to the nurses' station. I said to them, 'Do you
know what you're missing?' I told them to stop what they were
doing, to put everything aside, and come right down to the Activities Room."

Alas, she was not heeded. "I suppose some of those papers
piled on their desks are important too," she says, "but I didn't want
them to miss the Mozart."

As the group begins to leave for their noon meal, Jean pauses at
the door.

"Great today, Mary! How did that young musician do it? What
a contribution to the world!"

"I know," I say. "That Mozart—really extraordinary, wasn't
he?"

"Oh, I don't mean him," she says. "I mean the guy who wrote the words to *Mame*.

I do believe I detect a barely concealed glance of mirthful disbelief passing between Lydia and Fred. I wonder, does Fred smile because he understands the humor of Jean's remark or because he seems always to smile when he is with Lydia?

Meanwhile the World Goes On

I HEAR THESE WORDS as I approach Hannah, who is slowly pushing her walker toward her room in the Assisted Living Wing.

> You do not have to walk on your knees
> for a hundred miles through the desert, repenting.

"Poetry, Hannah! You remember!"

"'Wild Geese.' Oh yes, Mary Oliver is one of my favorites. I love her poetry."

Hannah continues remembering.

> Tell me about despair, yours, and I will tell you mine.
> Meanwhile the world goes on...

Hannah sometimes forgets things that the rest of us consider important. She may forget to get dressed before she walks down the hall in the morning. She may forget about having a young grandson. But shortly afterwards she tells me,

"Yesterday my grandson came to visit. He said to me, 'I love you, Grandma.'"

I say, "Oh, Hannah. What could be better than that!"

"Nothing."
She smiles and sits in silence for a long time.

A few days ago Hannah told me that her daughter, Isabel, living
in Chicago, had been hospitalized. An accident, she was told, but
Hannah knows nothing about her condition. On the following
day there is still sadness in her eyes. I ask her how she is doing.
"I don't know," she tells me, "I haven't had time to process it yet."

And then, this morning, Hannah excitedly beckons me in her
direction. "Isabel's going to be all right," she says. "We talked on
the phone a long time." I ask her what they talked about. "Well,
first it was about how she was feeling and what the doctor said.
After that," she chuckles, "we recited Mary Oliver to each other.
Isabel likes her too."

No longer so worried about her daughter, Hannah once again
feels free to pay attention to what is beautiful. She pauses in the
middle of a Mary Oliver essay. "Oh what a fine word. Even in her
prose, it's really poetry, isn't it?"

Hannah expresses a reverence for the arts. She believes that
those who don't honor a wonderful book of poetry must not be
offered the book. They will dishonor it by their lack of appreciation. "Books have feelings too, you know."

She respects everything around her—a person sitting next to
her, a character in a song, a dog. Often in our Mostly Music group
sessions, I ask for requests, for favorites. Hannah asks for Mary
Oliver's poem about her dog, "Percy Speaks While I Am Doing
Taxes."

> . . . *Just because*
> *I can't count to ten doesn't mean*
> *I don't remember yesterday, or anticipate today.*
> *I give you one more hour, then we step out*
> *into the beautiful money-deaf gift of the world*
> *and run.*

Percy's dog wisdom is not lost on our group. They ask for encores, for more poems. So now in my carrier, along with my CD music collection, I include a thin Mary Oliver book.

I tell Hannah how much I value what she said about books having feelings too.

"Oh, did I say that?"

"Yes, you did."

"Well, good for me."

Hannah's first choice for a musical selection is George Gershwin's "I Loves You, Porgy," from *Porgy and Bess*—the story about the unfortunate Bess who is abandoned by Crown, her violent lover, now hiding from the police for murder. We all want Bess to stay with Porgy, the handicapped beggar who has shown her compassion and kindness. Bess loves Porgy and says she would choose him, if possible, but when Crown returns, she knows she will have to go.

We all groan at those words. Why does she have to go? Why can't she stay with Porgy?

"But wait," Hannah tells us, "let's not judge her so quickly." She asks us to think about what Bess's life has always been, how she has learned to live the only way she knows, following that man in her life. Bess is pleading, but Bess needs to go—the difficult un-choice of so many women in her culture—and, Hannah adds, "in our culture as well."

Hannah has a way of getting us to think about our longings, about the truth of our own lives.

"I Loves You, Porgy" is no longer just another achingly sweet melody.

Hannah wants to continue the conversation later. She talks to me about the time before women were permitted to vote. She supposes that men thought the woman's vote wasn't necessary. What would women know about what was going on in the world anyway? Then with a twinkle in her eye, she adds, "Adam and Eve came into life about the same time. He didn't know any more than she did."

Time with Hannah becomes more and more precious. Her matter-of-fact insights about books and women, their choices and their rights, invariably leave me with something compelling to rethink, to discuss further. So I am especially distressed when I stop by Hannah's room on a Monday morning and am told that she was admitted to the hospital over the weekend. A possible stroke.

As I enter her hospital room, I see that she is surrounded by several young interns. I wait by the door.

"I would like to ask you another question," one of the doctors is saying.

"Yes."

"Do you know why you are here?"

"I'm here because *you* think I'm sick."

No one pauses at this response. Does no one hear her?

After a few days it is determined that Hannah did have a stroke. She is able to speak, but in need of therapy for her left arm and leg, until she can walk safely with a walker.

Her rehabilitation takes several weeks at a nearby facility. I watch as a physical therapist helps Hannah and a male resident with exercises, to strengthen their arms and legs. Hannah takes a long look at the man's effort to return a light beach ball on a bounce. She whispers to me, "Oh, how difficult it must be for a man not to be able to do these simple things, to have to be so sedentary." No mention of herself.

Although occupational therapy is wearisome, Hannah keeps occupied with other matters. She talks about life after death. "What do you think, Mary? Do you believe in it?"

"In my next life," I say, "I want to garden and to dance."

"But you have to do something about it *now*. You can only proceed with where you want to go next if you move in that direction *now*. You have to work at what you want to have happen."

— · —

Finally Hannah regains enough leg and arm strength to return to our senior community. I greet her the day after her return.

"Hannah, you're here! You're back! I'm so glad to see you."

"Now that I see you, I know that I am back."

She talks about the changes—her new room in the Skilled Nursing Facility, having to get used to the different aides assigned to her.

"They don't listen to what you say. You can tell from the way they answer you, or don't answer you."

A few minutes later she says, "This community we live in, it's a good place, a very generous place."

After a few weeks, Hannah once again becomes a part of our music group. We are listening to a recording of Paul Robeson singing "Ol' Man River," Jerome Kern's stirring song from *Showboat.*

You and me we sweat and strain
Body all achin' and racked wid pain…
Ah's tired of livin'
An skeered of dyin'…

When the song is over there is silence. I think the soul-wrenching lyrics and music have moved us to a deeper self.

And then, our Mostly Music group wants to know, *Who is this old man river? Is it a person? What is old man river? Not a river? Not a river? Slaves maybe?*

Many in the group begin to mention the slave. It's got to be the slave, the cruel, endless lot of the slave.

Hannah agrees with everything the group has been saying about the slave and the river. "But the river," they ask, "is it really a river?"

"I suppose it can be," says Hannah. "How could any slave not be longing for the crossing of the Jordan?"

The group waits for more from Hannah. "I think," she says, "it is pain. It is weariness, fear. And there is also pride and defiance. For me, 'Ol' Man River' is a metaphor for one's life—it is just keeping on and rolling along."

Afterword

IN THE LAST twelve years, I have accompanied our residents as they experienced losses, one after another. And yet, as they listen to music and listen to each other there is so much heart. They move me to consider again their lives and mine, and to be grateful for the fullness.

> *If you want to talk about this*
> *come to visit. I live in the house*
> *near the corner, which I have named*
> Gratitude
> —Mary Oliver

Acknowledgments

I wish to thank—

Clare Morris, who realized probably before I did that listening to music with the residents would make a difference in their lives and mine, for her heartening encouragement and thoughtful responses to each story. Thank you for nudging me to put them down on paper.

Donna Hardy and Clare Morris' Camp Writing Bear offerings at Angela Center, a place of inspiration and support, where I learned that "there is more to writing than writing."

John and Susan Daniel, publishers, for their encouragement, generous editorial advice and kindly guidance in what was for me an unknown world.

My first readers, who shared their caring, wisdom and laughter as they read along with me: Chrisie Kuno, for believing in the messages of my stories; Eunice Haas, for cheering me on year after year; Don Drury, the *Scribble and Sketch* staff, and members of my senior community for their ongoing help and support; and to Sister Jake who accompanied me from the conformity of our early school days into the uncharted territory of our elder years. Many thanks for reading my stories and asking for more.

Those wonderful few in my childhood who never read anything I ever wrote but made and continue to make a difference—

Uncle Pete, on what was for me a fairyland Santa Rosa farm

every summer after Mama died, who told me about irrigation, and apple trees, cows, geese, and chickens, and that I could do anything.

Mama, sitting next to me on the sunny brick steps behind the little iron gate, nudging me in Greek, her native language, to carry one of the grocery bags for the little old lady walking up our hill. "And remember, not to let her give you anything, not even a penny." Her warm smile as I ran back to her, watching for me by the gate.

Betty Howell, for reading every draft with a critical and loving eye; for endless enthusiasm, for knowing when there was something more that needed to be said, or something less. Thank you for making every reading session a source of renewed writing energy and joy—and for our blessed friendship.

My husband Wally, for his love that continues to sustain me. Although Wally will not read my stories as others do, in some mysterious way he has contributed to each of our music-listening sessions and to the writing of *A Song Just for Me*. I am grateful all the time.

Jerry Anderson

MARY KIKI WILCOX

As a young child Mary was blessed with a deeply engaged violin teacher who created string groups for beginning pupils, nudging them into taking each others' parts so they could hear and appreciate the inner voices. She remembers the joy of breathing and listening together with her teen-age quartet, which continued to play as a group into their thirties. She married and found herself in the role of stepmother and needing, she says, all of the listening skills she could muster.

Mary has a Ph.D. from Stanford University, was a teacher and principal in the San Francisco public schools, and senior education researcher at SRI International. She lives in Palo Alto, California.